Charles George Douglas Roberts

Songs of the Common Day

and Ave! - an Ode for the Shelley Centenary

Charles George Douglas Roberts

Songs of the Common Day

and Ave! - an Ode for the Shelley Centenary

ISBN/EAN: 9783337179885

Printed in Europe, USA, Canada, Australia, Japan

Cover: Foto ©Lupo / pixelio.de

More available books at **www.hansebooks.com**

SONGS OF THE COMMON DAY

By the same Author

ORION, AND OTHER POEMS [*Out of print*

IN DIVERS TONES   [*D. Lothrop Company*

THE CANADIANS OF OLD
   (From the French of PHILIPPE AUBERT DE GASPÉ)
              D. Appleton & Co.

THE CANADIAN GUIDE-BOOK
         New York: D. Appleton & Co.

SONGS
OF THE COMMON DAY

AND

AVE!

AN ODE FOR THE SHELLEY CENTENARY

BY

CHARLES G. D. ROBERTS

LONDON
LONGMANS, GREEN, AND CO.
AND NEW YORK : 15 EAST 16th STREET
1893

All rights reserved

TO

BLISS CARMAN

FRIEND, KINSMAN, AND FELLOW CRAFTSMAN

PREFATORY NOTE

By the kind courtesy of Messrs. D. Lothrop Company, I am permitted to reprint in this collection seven sonnets from my volume entitled 'In Divers Tones.' This is done to complete the series of sonnets dealing with aspects of common outdoor life. The sonnets reprinted are 'The Sower,' 'The Potato Harvest,' 'Tides,' 'In September,' 'Dark,' 'Rain,' and 'Mist.' The Ode for the Centenary of Shelley's Birth was first published by the Williamson Book Company, of Toronto, in December 1892, in a limited edition of two hundred copies.

C. G. D. R.

KINGSCROFT, WINDSOR, N.S., CANADA :
May 1893.

CONTENTS

	PAGE
'ACROSS THE FOG THE MOON LIES FAIR'.	1

SONNETS

THE FURROW	2
THE SOWER	3
THE WAKING EARTH	4
THE COW PASTURE	5
WHEN MILKING-TIME IS DONE	6
FROGS	7
THE SALT FLATS	8
THE FIR WOODS	9
THE PEA-FIELDS	10
THE MOWING	11
BURNT LANDS	12
THE CLEARING	13
THE SUMMER POOL	14
BUCKWHEAT	15
THE CICADA IN THE FIRS	16

CONTENTS

	PAGE
IN SEPTEMBER	17
A VESPER SONNET	18
THE POTATO HARVEST	19
THE OAT-THRESHING	20
THE AUTUMN THISTLES	21
INDIAN SUMMER	22
THE PUMPKINS IN THE CORN	23
THE WINTER FIELDS	24
IN AN OLD BARN	25
MIDWINTER THAW	26
THE FLIGHT OF THE GEESE	27
IN THE WIDE AWE AND WISDOM OF THE NIGHT	28
THE HERRING WEIR	29
BLOMIDON	30
THE NIGHT SKY	31
TIDES	32
THE DESERTED CITY	33
DARK	34
RAIN	35
MIST	36
MOONLIGHT	37
O SOLITARY OF THE AUSTERE SKY	38

POEMS

AUTOCHTHON	39
THE TIDE ON TANTRAMAR	42
THE VALLEY OF THE WINDING WATER	51
MARSYAS	52

CONTENTS

	PAGE
THE FORTRESS	54
SEVERANCE	55
EPITAPH FOR A SAILOR BURIED ASHORE	56
THE SILVER THAW	57
THE LILY OF THE VALLEY	60
THE NIGHT-HAWK	61
THE HERMIT-THRUSH	63
THE WILD-ROSE THICKET	65
MY TREES	66
THE HAWKBIT	67
GREY ROCKS AND GREYER SEA	68
A SONG OF CHEER	69
A SONG OF GROWTH	71
TO G. B. R.	73
THE BIRD'S SONG, THE SUN, AND THE WIND	74
OH, PURPLE HANG THE PODS	75
BRINGING HOME THE COWS	76
THE KEEPERS OF THE PASS	78
NEW YEAR'S EVE (*After the French of Fréchette*)	81
A CHRISTMAS-EVE COURTIN'	84
THE SUCCOUR OF GLUSKÂP	91
HOW THE MOHAWKS SET OUT FOR MEDOCTEC	95
THE WOOD FROLIC	100
CANADIAN STREAMS	105

AVE! AN ODE FOR THE CENTENARY OF SHELLEY'S BIRTH 111

Across the fog the moon lies fair.
    Transfused with ghostly amethyst,
O white Night, charm to wonderment
    The cattle in the mist !

Thy touch, O grave Mysteriarch,
    Makes dull, familiar things divine.
O grant of thy revealing gift
    Be some small portion mine !

Make thou my vision sane and clear,
    That I may see what beauty clings
In common forms, and find the soul
    Of unregarded things !

THE FURROW

How sombre slope these acres to the sea
   And to the breaking sun ! The sun-rise deeps
   Of rose and crocus, whence the far dawn leaps,
Gild but with scorn their grey monotony.
The glebe rests patient for its joy to be.
   Past the salt field-foot many a dim wing sweeps ;
   And down the field a first slow furrow creeps,
Pledge of near harvests to the unverdured lea.

With clank of harness tramps the serious team—
   The sea air thrills their nostrils. Some wise crows
   Feed confidently behind the ploughman's feet.
In the early chill the clods fresh cloven steam,
   And down its griding path the keen share goes :
   So, from a scar, best flowers the future's sweet.

THE SOWER

A BROWN, sad-coloured hillside, where the soil
   Fresh from the frequent harrow, deep and fine,
   Lies bare ; no break in the remote sky-line,
Save where a flock of pigeons streams aloft,
Startled from feed in some low-lying croft,
   Or far-off spires with yellow of sunset shine ;
   And here the Sower, unwittingly divine,
Exerts the silent forethought of his toil.

Alone he treads the glebe, his measured stride
   Dumb in the yielding soil ; and though small joy
   Dwell in his heavy face, as spreads the blind
Pale grain from his dispensing palm aside,
   This plodding churl grows great in his employ ;—
   Godlike, he makes provision for mankind.

THE WAKING EARTH

With shy bright clamour the live brooks sparkle and run.
Freed flocks confer about the farmstead ways.
The air's a wine of dreams and shining haze,
Beaded with bird-notes thin,—for Spring's begun !
The sap flies upward. Death is over and done.
    The glad earth wakes ; the glad light breaks ; the days
    Grow round, grow radiant. Praise for the new life !
        Praise
For bliss of breath and blood beneath the sun !

What potent wizardry the wise earth wields,
To conjure with a perfume ! From bare fields
    The sense drinks in a breath of furrow and sod.
And lo, the bound of days and distance yields ;
    And fetterless the soul is flown abroad,
    Lord of desire and beauty, like a God !

THE COW PASTURE

I see the harsh, wind-ridden, eastward hill,
   By the red cattle pastured, blanched with dew ;
   The small, mossed hillocks where the clay gets
      through ;
The grey webs woven on milkweed tops at will.
The sparse, pale grasses flicker, and are still.
   The empty flats yearn seaward. All the view
   Is naked to the horizon's utmost blue ;
And the bleak spaces stir me with strange thrill.

Not in perfection dwells the subtler power
   To pierce our mean content, but rather works
   Through incompletion, and the need that irks,—
Not in the flower, but effort toward the flower.
   When the want stirs, when the soul's cravings urge,
   The strong earth strengthens, and the clean
      heavens purge.

WHEN MILKING-TIME IS DONE

When milking-time is done, and over all
   This quiet Canadian inland forest home
   And wide rough pasture-lots the shadows come,
And dews, with peace and twilight voices, fall,
From moss-cooled watering-trough to foddered stall
   The tired plough-horses turn,—the barnyard loam
   Soft to their feet,—and in the sky's pale dome
Like resonant chords the swooping night-jars call.

The frogs, cool-fluting ministers of dream,
   Make shrill the slow brook's borders ; pasture bars
   Down clatter, and the cattle wander through,—
Vague shapes amid the thickets ; gleam by gleam
   Above the wet grey wilds emerge the stars,
   And through the dusk the farmstead fades from view.

FROGS

HERE in the red heart of the sunset lying,
   My rest an islet of brown weeds blown dry,
   I watch the wide bright heavens, hovering nigh,
My plain and pools in lucent splendours dyeing.
My view dreams over the rosy wastes, descrying
   The reed-tops fret the solitary sky ;
   And all the air is tremulous to the cry
Of myriad frogs on mellow pipes replying.

For the unrest of passion here is peace,
   And eve's cool drench for midday soil and taint.
To tired ears how sweetly brings release
   This limpid babble from life's unstilled complaint ;
While under tired eyelids lapse and faint
The noon's derisive visions—fade and cease.

THE SALT FLATS

HERE clove the keels of centuries ago
   Where now unvisited the flats lie bare.
   Here seethed the sweep of journeying waters, where
No more the tumbling floods of Fundy flow,
And only in the samphire pipes creep slow
   The salty currents of the sap.   The air
   Hums desolately with wings that seaward fare,
Over the lonely reaches beating low.

The wastes of hard and meagre weeds are thronged
With murmurs of a past that time has wronged ;
   And ghosts of many an ancient memory
Dwell by the brackish pools and ditches blind,
In these low-lying pastures of the wind,
   These marshes pale and meadows by the sea.

THE FIR WOODS

The wash of endless waves is in their tops,
  Endlessly swaying, and the long winds stream
  Athwart them from the far-off shores of dream.
Through the stirred branches filtering, faintly drops
Mystic dream-dust of isle, and palm, and cave,
  Coral and sapphire, realms of rose, that seem
  More radiant than ever earthly gleam
Revealed of fairy mead or haunted wave.

A cloud of gold, a cleft of blue profound,—
  These are my gates of wonder, surged about
  By tumult of tossed bough and rocking crest :
The vision lures. The spirit spurns her bound,
  Spreads her unprisoned wing, and drifts from out
  This green and humming gloom that wraps my rest.

THE PEA-FIELDS

These are the fields of light, and laughing air,
   And yellow butterflies, and foraging bees,
   And whitish, wayward blossoms winged as these,
And pale green tangles like a seamaid's hair.
Pale, pale the blue, but pure beyond compare,
   And pale the sparkle of the far-off seas,
   A-shimmer like these fluttering slopes of peas,
And pale the open landscape everywhere.

From fence to fence a perfumed breath exhales
   O'er the bright pallor of the well-loved fields,—
My fields of Tantramar in summer-time;
   And, scorning the poor feed their pasture yields,
Up from the bushy lots the cattle climb,
   To gaze with longing through the grey, mossed rails.

THE MOWING

THIS is the voice of high midsummer's heat.
  The rasping vibrant clamour soars and shrills
  O'er all the meadowy range of shadeless hills,
As if a host of giant cicadae beat
The cymbals of their wings with tireless feet,
  Or brazen grasshoppers with triumphing note
  From the long swath proclaimed the fate that smote
The clover and timothy-tops and meadowsweet.

The crying knives glide on ; the green swath lies.
  And all noon long the sun, with chemic ray,
  Seals up each cordial essence in its cell,
That in the dusky stalls, some winter's day,
  The spirit of June, here prisoned by his spell,
  May cheer the herds with pasture memories.

BURNT LANDS

On other fields and other scenes the morn
   Laughs from her blue,—but not such fields are these,
   Where comes no cheer of summer leaves and bees,
And no shade mitigates the day's white scorn.
These serious acres vast no groves adorn ;
   But giant trunks, bleak shapes that once were trees,
   Tower naked, unassuaged of rain or breeze,
Their stern grey isolation grimly borne.

The months roll over them, and mark no change.
   But when Spring stirs, or Autumn stills, the year,
   Perchance some phantom leafage rustles faint
Through their parched dreams,—some old-time notes
     ring strange,
   When in his slender treble, far and clear,
   Reiterates the rain-bird his complaint.

THE CLEARING

STUMPS, and harsh rocks, and prostrate trunks all charred.
 And gnarled roots naked to the sun and rain,—
 They seem in their grim stillness to complain,
And by their plaint the evening peace is jarred.
These ragged acres fire and the axe have scarred,
 And many summers not assuaged their pain.
 In vain the pink and saffron light, in vain
The pale dew on the hillocks stripped and marred !

But here and there the waste is touched with cheer
 Where spreads the fire-weed like a crimson flood
And venturous plumes of golden-rod appear ;
 And round the blackened fence the great boughs lean
With comfort ; and across the solitude
 The hermit's holy transport peals serene.

THE SUMMER POOL

This is a wonder-cup in Summer's hand.
   Sombre, impenetrable, round its rim
   The fir-trees bend and brood.   The noons o'erbrim
The windless hollow of its iris'd strand
With mote-thick sun and water-breathings bland.
   Under a veil of lilies lurk and swim
   Strange shapes of presage in a twilight dim,
Unwitting heirs of light and life's command.

Blind in their bondage, of no change they dream,
   But the trees watch in grave expectancy
   The spell fulfils,—and swarms of radiant flame,
Live jewels, above the crystal dart and gleam,
   Nor guess the sheen beneath their wings to be
   The dark and narrow regions whence they came.

BUCKWHEAT

This smell of home and honey on the breeze,
   This shimmer of sunshine woven in white and pink
   That comes, a dream from memory's visioned brink,
Sweet, sweet and strange across the ancient trees, --
It is the buckwheat, boon of the later bees,
   Its breadths of heavy-headed bloom appearing
   Amid the blackened stumps of this high clearing,
Freighted with cheer of comforting auguries.

But when the blunt, brown grain and red-ripe sheaves,
Brimming the low log barn beyond the eaves,
   Crisped by the first frost, feel the thresher's flail,
Then flock the blue wild-pigeons in shy haste
   All silently down Autumn's amber trail,
To glean at dawn the chill and whitening waste.

THE CICADA IN THE FIRS

CHARM of the vibrant, white September sun—
  How tower the firs to take it, tranced and still !
  Their scant ranks crown the pale, round, pasture-hill,
And watch, far down, the austere waters run
Their circuit thro' the serious marshes dun.
  No bird-call stirs the blue ; but strangely thrill
  The blunt-faced, brown cicada's wing-notes shrill,
A web of silver o'er the silence spun.

O zithern-winged musician, whence it came,
  I wonder, this insistent song of thine !
  Did once the highest string of Summer's lyre,
Snapt on some tense chord slender as a flame,
  Take form again in these vibrations fine
  That o'er the tranquil spheres of noon aspire ?

IN SEPTEMBER

THIS windy, bright September afternoon
My heart is wide awake, yet full of dreams.
The air, alive with hushed confusion, teems
With scent of grain-fields, and a mystic rune,
Foreboding of the fall of Summer soon,
    Keeps swelling and subsiding ; till there seems
    O'er all the world of valleys, hills, and streams,
Only the wind's inexplicable tune.

My heart is full of dreams, yet wide awake.
    I lie and watch the topmost tossing boughs
    Of tall elms, pale against the vaulted blue ;
But even now some yellowing branches shake,
    Some hue of death the living green endows :—
    If beauty flies, fain would I vanish too.

A VESPER SONNET

This violet eve is like a waveless stream
  Celestial, from the rapt horizon's brink,
  Assuaging day with the diviner drink
Of temperate ecstasy, and dews, and dream.
The wine-warm dusks, that brim the valley, gleam
  With here and there a lonely casement. Cease
  The impetuous purples from the sky of peace,
Like God's mood in tranquillity supreme.

The encircling uplands east and west lie clear
  In thin aërial amber, threaded fine,—
Where bush-fires gnaw the bramble-thickets sere,
  With furtive scarlet. Through the hush benign
One white-throat voices, till the stars appear,
  The benediction of the Thought Divine.

THE POTATO HARVEST

A HIGH bare field, brown from the plough, and borne
   Aslant from sunset ; amber wastes of sky
   Washing the ridge ; a clamour of crows that fly
In from the wide flats where the spent tides mourn
To yon their rocking roosts in pines wind-torn ;
   A line of grey snake-fence, that zigzags by
   A pond, and cattle ; from the homestead nigh
The long deep summonings of the supper horn.

Black on the ridge, against that lonely flush,
   A cart, and stoop-necked oxen ; ranged beside
   Some barrels ; and the day-worn harvest-folk,
Here emptying their baskets, jar the hush
   With hollow thunders. Down the dusk hillside
   Lumbers the wain ; and day fades out like smoke.

THE OAT-THRESHING

A LITTLE brown old homestead, bowered in trees
   That o'er the Autumn landscape shine afar,
   Burning with amber and with cinnabar.
A yellow hillside washed in airy seas
Of azure, where the swallow drops and flees.
   Midway the slope, clear in the beaming day,
   A barn by many seasons beaten grey,
Big with the gain of prospering husbandries.

In billows round the wide red welcoming doors
   High piles the golden straw ; while from within,
   Where plods the team amid the chaffy din,
The loud pulsation of the thresher soars,
   Persistent as if earth could not let cease
   This happy proclamation of her peace.

THE AUTUMN THISTLES

THE morning sky is white with mist, the earth
  White with the inspiration of the dew.
  The harvest light is on the hills anew,
And cheer in the grave acres' fruitful girth.
Only in this high pasture is there dearth,
  Where the gray thistles crowd in ranks austere,
  As if the sod, close-cropt for many a year,
Brought only bane and bitterness to birth.

But in the crisp air's amethystine wave
  How the harsh stalks are washed with radiance now,
  How gleams the harsh turf where the crickets lie
Dew-freshened in their burnished armour brave !
  Since earth could not endure nor heaven allow
  Aught of unlovely in the morn's clear eye.

INDIAN SUMMER

WHAT touch hath set the breathing hills afire
   With amethyst, to quench them with a tear
   Of ecstasy? These common fields appear
The consecrated home of hopes past number.
So many visions, so entranced a slumber,
   Such dreams possess the noonday's luminous sphere,
   That earth, content with knowing Heaven so near,
Hath done with aspiration and desire.

In these unlooked-for hours of Truth's clear reign
   Unjarring fitness hath surprised our strife.
This radiance, that might seem to cheat the view
With loveliness too perfect to be true,
   But shows this vexed and self-delusive life
   Ideals whereto our Real must attain.

THE PUMPKINS IN THE CORN

AMBER and blue, the smoke behind the hill,
  Where in the glow fades out the Morning Star,
  Curtains the Autumn cornfield, sloped afar,
And strikes an acrid savour on the chill.
The hilltop fence shines saffron o'er the still
  Unbending ranks of bunched and bleaching corn
  And every pallid stalk is crisp with morn,
Crisp with the silver Autumn morn's distil.

Purple the narrowing alleys stretched between
  The spectral shooks, a purple harsh and cold,
  But spotted, where the gadding pumpkins run,
With bursts of blaze that startle the serene
  Like sudden voices,—globes of orange bold,
  Elate to mimic the unrisen sun.

THE WINTER FIELDS

WINDS here, and sleet, and frost that bites like steel.
   The low bleak hill rounds under the low sky.
   Naked of flock and fold the fallows lie,
Thin streaked with meagre drift. The gusts reveal
By fits the dim grey snakes of fence, that steal
   Through the white dusk. The hill-foot poplars sigh,
   While storm and death with winter trample by,
And the iron fields ring sharp, and blind lights reel.

Yet in the lonely ridges, wrenched with pain,
   Harsh solitary hillocks, bound and dumb,
Grave glebes close-lipped beneath the scourge and chain,
   Lurks hid the germ of ecstasy—the sum
Of life that waits on summer, till the rain
   Whisper in April and the crocus come.

IN AN OLD BARN

Tons upon tons the brown-green fragrant hay
   O'erbrims the mows beyond the time-warped eaves,
   Up to the rafters where the spider weaves,
Though few flies wander his secluded way.
Through a high chink one lonely golden ray,
   Wherein the dust is dancing, slants unstirred.
   In the dry hush some rustlings light are heard,
Of winter-hidden mice at furtive play.

Far down, the cattle in their shadowed stalls,
   Nose-deep in clover fodder's meadowy scent,
   Forget the snows that whelm their pasture streams,
The frost that bites the world beyond their walls.
   Warm housed, they dream of summer, well content
   In day-long contemplation of their dreams.

MIDWINTER THAW

How shrink the snows upon this upland field,
   Under the dove-grey dome of brooding noon !
   They shrink with soft, reluctant shocks, and soon
In sad brown ranks the furrows lie revealed.
From radiant cisterns of the frost unsealed
   Now wakes through all the air a watery rune—
   The babble of a million brooks atune,
In fairy conduits of blue ice concealed.

Noisy with crows, the wind-break on the hill
   Counts o'er its buds for summer.   In the air
Some shy foreteller prophesies with skill—
   Some voyaging ghost of bird, some effluence rare ;
And the stall-wearied cattle dream their fill
   Of deep June pastures where the pools are fair.

THE FLIGHT OF THE GEESE

I HEAR the low wind wash the softening snow,
   The low tide loiter down the shore. The night
   Full filled with April forecast, hath no light.
The salt wave on the sedge-flat pulses slow.
Through the hid furrows lisp in murmurous flow
   The thaw's shy ministers ; and hark ! The height
   Of heaven grows weird and loud with unseen flight
Of strong hosts prophesying as they go !

High through the drenched and hollow night their wings
   Beat northward hard on winter's trail. The sound
Of their confused and solemn voices, borne
Athwart the dark to their long Arctic morn,
   Comes with a sanction and an awe profound,
A boding of unknown, foreshadowed things.

IN THE WIDE AWE AND WISDOM OF THE NIGHT

IN the wide awe and wisdom of the night
    I saw the round world rolling on its way,
Beyond significance of depth or height,
    Beyond the interchange of dark and day.
I marked the march to which is set no pause,
    And that stupendous orbit, round whose rim
The great sphere sweeps, obedient unto laws
    That utter the eternal thought of Him.
I compassed time, outstripped the starry speed,
    And in my still soul apprehended space,
Till, weighing laws which these but blindly heed,
    At last I came before Him face to face,—
And knew the Universe of no such span
As the august infinitude of Man.

THE HERRING WEIR

BACK to the green deeps of the outer bay
  The red and amber currents glide and cringe,
  Diminishing behind a luminous fringe
Of cream-white surf and wandering wraiths of spray.
Stealthily, in the old reluctant way,
  The red flats are uncovered, mile on mile,
  To glitter in the sun a golden while.
Far down the flats, a phantom sharply gray,
The herring weir emerges, quick with spoil.
  Slowly the tide forsakes it. Then draws near,
  Descending from the farm-house on the height,
A cart, with gaping tubs. The oxen toil
  Sombrely o'er the level to the weir,
  And drag a long black trail across the light.

BLOMIDON

This is that black rock bastion, based in surge,
    Pregnant with agate and with amethyst,
Whose foot the tides of storied Minas scourge,
    Whose top austere withdraws into its mist.
This is that ancient cape of tears and storm,
    Whose towering front inviolable frowns
O'er vales Evangeline and love keep warm—
    Whose fame thy song, O tender singer, crowns.
Yonder, across these reeling fields of foam,
    Came the sad threat of the avenging ships.
What profit now to know if just the doom,
    Though harsh! The streaming eyes, the praying lips,
The shadow of inextinguishable pain,
The poet's deathless music—these remain!

THE NIGHT SKY

O DEEP of Heaven, 'tis thou alone art boundless,
  'Tis thou alone our balance shall not weigh,
'Tis thou alone our fathom-line finds soundless,—
  Whose infinite our finite must obey !
Through thy blue realms and down thy starry reaches
  Thought voyages forth beyond the furthest fire,
And, homing from no sighted shoreline, teaches
  Thee measureless as is the soul's desire.
O deep of Heaven, no beam of Pleiad ranging
  Eternity may bridge thy gulf of spheres !
The ceaseless hum that fills thy sleep unchanging
  Is rain of the innumerable years.
Our worlds, our suns, our ages, these but stream
Through thine abiding like a dateless dream.

TIDES

THROUGH the still dusk how sighs the ebb-tide out
    Reluctant for the reed-beds ! Down the sands
    It washes. Hark ! Beyond the wan grey strand's
Low limits how the winding channels grieve,
Aware the evasive waters soon will leave
    Them void amid the waste of desolate lands,
    Where shadowless to the sky the marsh expands,
And the noon heats must scar them, and the drought.

Yet soon for them the solacing tide returns
    To quench their thirst of longing. Ah, not so
Works the stern law our tides of life obey !
Ebbing in the night watches swift away,
    Scarce known are fled for ever is the flow ;
And in parched channel still the shrunk stream mourns.

THE DESERTED CITY

THERE lies a little city leagues away.
   Its wharves the green sea washes all day long.
   Its busy, sun-bright wharves with sailors' song
And clamour of trade ring loud the live-long day.
Into the happy harbour hastening, gay
   With press of snowy canvas, tall ships throng.
   The peopled streets to blithe-eyed Peace belong,
Glad housed beneath these crowding roofs of grey.

'Twas long ago this city prospered so,
   For yesterday a woman died therein.
Since when the wharves are idle fallen, I know,
   And in the streets is hushed the pleasant din ;
   The thronging ships have been, the songs have been ;—
Since yesterday it is so long ago.

DARK

Now, for the night is hushed and blind with rain,
  My soul desires communion, Dear, with thee.
  But hour by hour my spirit gets not free,—
Hour by still hour my longing strives in vain.
The thick dark hems me, even to the restless brain.
  The wind's confusion vague encumbers me.
  Even passionate memory, grown too faint to see
Thy features, stirs not in her straitening chain.

And thou, dost thou too feel this strange divorce
  Of will from power? The spell of night and wind,
  Baffling desire and dream, dost thou too find?
Not distance parts us, Dear; but this dim force,
  Intangible, holds us helpless, hushed with pain,
  Dumb with the dark, blind with the gusts of rain!

RAIN

SHARP drives the rain, sharp drives the endless rain.
   The rain-winds wake and wander, lift and blow.
   The slow smoke-wreaths of vapour to and fro,
Wave and unweave and gather and build again.
Over the far gray reaches of the plain, —
   Grey miles on miles my passionate thought must go, —
   I strain my sight, grown dim with gazing so,
Pressing my face against the streaming pane.

How the rain beats! Ah God! If love had power
   To voice its utmost yearning, even tho'
   Through time and bitter distance, not in vain,
Surely her heart would hear me at this hour,
   Look through the years, and see! But would she know
The white face pressed against the streaming pane?

MIST

Its hand compassionate guards our restless sight
  Against how many a harshness, many an ill !
  Tender as sleep, its shadowy palms distil
Weird vapours that ensnare our eyes with light.
Rash eyes, kept ignorant in their own despite,
  It lets not see the unsightliness they will,
  But paints each scanty fairness fairer still,
And still deludes us to our own delight.

It fades, regathers, never quite dissolves.
  And, ah ! that life, ah ! that the heart and brain
  Might keep their mist and glamour, not to know
So soon the disenchantment and the pain !
  But one by one our dear illusions go,
Stript and cast forth as time's slow wheel revolves.

MOONLIGHT

THE fifers of these amethystine fields,
  Whose far fine sound the night makes musical,
  Now while thou wak'st and longing would'st recall
Joys that no rapture of remembrance yields,
Voice to thy soul, lone-sitting deep within
  The still recesses of thine ecstasy,
  My love and my desire, that fain would fly
With this far-silvering moon and fold thee in.

But not for us the touch, the clasp, the kiss,
  And for our restlessness no rest. In vain
  These aching lips, these hungering hearts that strain
Toward the denied fruition of our bliss,
  Had love not learned of longing to devise
  Out of desire and dream our paradise.

O SOLITARY OF THE AUSTERE SKY

O SOLITARY of the austere sky,
    Pale presence of the unextinguished star,
That from thy station where the spheres wheel by,
    And quietudes of infinite patience are,
Watchest this wet, grey-visaged world emerge,—
    Cold pinnacle on pinnacle, and deep
On deep of ancient wood and wandering surge,—
    Out of the silence and the mists of sleep;

How small am I in thine august regard!
    Invisible,—and yet I know my worth!
When comes the hour to break this 'prisoning shard,
    And reunite with Him that breathed me forth,
Then shall this atom of the Eternal Soul
Encompass thee in its benign control!

AUTOCHTHON

I

I AM the spirit astir
To swell the grain
When fruitful suns confer
With labouring rain ;
I am the life that thrills
In branch and bloom ;
I am the patience of abiding hills,
The promise masked in doom.

II

When the sombre lands are wrung,
And storms are out,
And giant woods give tongue,
I am the shout ;

And when the earth would sleep,
    Wrapped in her snows,
I am the infinite gleam of eyes that keep
    The post of her repose.

III

I am the hush of calm,
    I am the speed,
The flood-tide's triumphing psalm,
    The marsh-pool's heed ;
I work in the rocking roar
    Where cataracts fall ;
I flash in the prismy fire that dances o'er
    The dew's ephemeral ball.

IV

I am the voice of wind
    And wave and tree,
Of stern desires and blind,
    Of strength to be ;
I am the cry by night
    At point of dawn,
The summoning bugle from the unseen height,
    In cloud and doubt withdrawn.

V

I am the strife that shapes
    The stature of man,
The pang no hero escapes,
    The blessing, the ban ;
I am the hammer that moulds
    The iron of our race,
The omen of God in our blood that a people beholds,
    The foreknowledge veiled in our face.

THE TIDE ON TANTRAMAR

I

TANTRAMAR! Tantramar!
I see thy cool green plains afar.
Thy dykes where grey sea-grasses are,
    Mine eyes behold them yet.

But not the gladness breathed of old
Thy bordering, blue hill-hollows hold;
Thy wind-blown leagues of green unrolled,
    Thy flats the red floods fret,

Thy steady-streaming winds—no more
These work the rapture wrought of yore,
When all thy wide bright strength outbore
    . My soul from fleshly bar.

A darkness as of drifted rain
Is over tide, and dyke, and plain.
The shadow-pall of human pain
   Is fallen on Tantramar.

II

A little garden gay with phlox,
Blue corn-flowers, yellow hollyhocks,
Red poppies, pink and purple stocks,
   Looks over Tantramar.

Pale yellow drops the road before
The hospitable cottage-door;—
A yellow, upland road, and o'er
The green marsh seeks the low red shore
   And winding dykes afar.

Beyond the marsh, and miles away,
The great tides of the tumbling bay
Swing glittering in the golden day,
   Swing foaming to and fro ;

And nearer, in a nest of green,
A little turbid port is seen,
Where pitch-black fishing-boats careen,
    Left when the tide runs low.

The little port is safe and fit.
About its wharf the plover flit,
The grey net-reels loom over it,
    With grass about their feet.

In wave and storm it hath no part,
This harbour in the marshes' heart ;
Behind its dykes, at peace, apart
    It hears the surges beat.

The garden hollyhocks are tall ;
They tower above the garden wall,
And see, far down, the port, and all
    The creeks, and marshes wide ;

But Margery, Margery,
'Tis something further thou wouldst see !
Bid all thy blooms keep watch with thee
    Across the outmost tide.

Bid them keep wide their starry eyes
To warn thee should a white sail rise,
Slow climbing up, from alien skies,
    The azure round of sea.

He sails beneath a stormy star;
The waves are wild, the Isles afar;
Summer is ripe on Tantramar,
    And yet returns not he.

Long, long thine eyes have watched in vain,
Waited in fear, and wept again.
Is it no more than lover's pain
    That makes thy heart so wild?

At dreams within the cottage door
The old man's eyes are lingering o'er
The little port,—the far-off shore,—
    His dear and only child.

And at her spinning-wheel within
The mother's hands forget to spin.
With loving voice she calls thee in,—
    Her dear and only child.

To leave the home-dear hearts to ache
Was not for thee, though thine should break.
For their dear sake, for their dear sake,
    Thou wouldst not go with him.

But always wise, and strong, and free,
Is given to which of us to be?—
A gathering shadow, Margery,
    Makes all thy daylight dim!

Yet surely soon will break the day
For which thine anxious waitings pray,—
His sails, athwart the yellow bay,
    Shall cleave the sky's blue rim.

III

To-night the wind roars in from sea;
The crow clings in the straining tree;
Curlew and crane and bittern flee
    The dykes of Tantramar.

To-night athwart an inky sky
A narrowing sun dropped angrily,
Scoring the gloom with dreadful dye,
    A bitter and flaming scar.

But ere night falls, across the tide
A close-reefed barque has been descried,
And word goes round the country-side—
    ' The " Belle " is in the bay ! '

And ere the loud night closes down
Upon that light's terrific frown,
Along the dyke, with blowing gown,
    She takes her eager way.

Just where his boat will haste to land,
On the open wharf she takes her stand.
Her pale hair blows from out its band.
    She does not heed the storm.

Her blinding joy of heart they know
Who so have fared, and waited so.
She heeds not what the winds that blow :
    She does not feel the storm.

But fiercer roars the gale. The night
With cloud grows black, with foam gleams white
The creek boils to its utmost height.
    The port is seething full.

The gale shouts in the outer waves
Amid a world of gaping graves ;
Against the dyke each great surge raves,
    Blind battering like a bull.

The dyke ! The dyke ! The brute sea shakes
The sheltering wall. It breaks,—it breaks !
The sharp salt whips her face, and wakes
    The dreamer from her dream.

The great flood lifts. It thunders in.
The broad marsh foams, and sinks. The din
Of waves is where her world has been ;—
    Is this—is this the dream ?

——One moment in that surging hell
The old wharf shook, then cringed and fell.
——Then came a lonely hulk, the ' Belle,'
    And drove athwart the waste.

  .   .   .   .   .   .

They know no light, nor any star,
Those ruined plains of Tantramar.
And where the maid and lover are
    They know nor fear nor haste.

IV

After the flood on Tantramar
The fisher-folk flocked in from far.
They stopped the breach ; they healed the scar.
    Once more the marsh grew green.

But at the marsh's inmost edge,
Where a tall fringe of flag and sedge
Catches a climbing hawthorn hedge,
    A lonely hulk is seen.

It lies forgotten of all tides,
The grass grows round its bleaching sides,
An endless inland peace abides
    About its mouldering age.

But in the cot-door on the height
An old man sits with fading sight,
And memories of one cruel night
    Are all his heritage.

And at her spinning-wheel within
The mother's hands forget to spin,—
So weary all her days have been
    Since Margery went away.

——Tantramar ! Tantramar !
Until that sorrow fades afar,
Thy plains where birds and blossoms are
    Laugh not their ancient way !

THE VALLEY OF THE WINDING WATER

THE valley of the winding water
　Wears the same light it wore of old.
Still o'er the purple peaks the portals
　Of distance and desire unfold.

Still break the fields of opening June
　To emerald in their ancient way.
The sapphire of the summer heaven
　Is infinite, as yesterday.

My eyes are on the greening earth,
　The exultant bobolinks wild awing;
And yet, of all this kindly gladness,
　My heart beholds not anything.

For in a still room far away,
　With mourners round her silent head,
Blind to the quenchless tears, the anguish—
　I see, to-day, a woman dead.

MARSYAS

A LITTLE grey hill-glade, close-turfed, withdrawn
Beyond resort or heed of trafficking feet,
Ringed round with slim trunks of the mountain ash.
Through the slim trunks and scarlet bunches flash—
Beneath the clear chill glitterings of the dawn—
Far off, the crests, where down the rosy shore
The Pontic surges beat.
The plains lie dim below. The thin airs wash
The circuit of the autumn-coloured hills,
And this high glade, whereon
The satyr pipes, who soon shall pipe no more.
He sits against the beech-tree's mighty bole,—
He leans, and with persuasive breathing fills
The happy shadows of the slant-set lawn.
The goat-feet fold beneath a gnarlèd root ;
And sweet, and sweet the note that steals and thrills
From slender stops of that shy flute.
Then to the goat-feet comes the wide-eyed fawn

Hearkening ; the rabbits fringe the glade, and lay
Their long ears to the sound ;
In the pale boughs the partridge gather round,
And quaint hern from the sea-green river reeds ;
The wild ram halts upon a rocky horn
O'erhanging ; and, unmindful of his prey,
The leopard steals with narrowed lids to lay
His spotted length along the ground.
The thin airs wash, the thin clouds wander by,
And those hushed listeners move not. All the morn
He pipes, soft-swaying, and with half-shut eye,
In rapt content of utterance,—
      nor heeds
The young God standing in his branchy place,
The languor on his lips, and in his face,
Divinely inaccessible, the scorn.

THE FORTRESS

WHILE raves the midnight storm,
And roars the rain upon the windy roof,
Heart held to heart and all the world aloof,
We laugh secure and warm.

This chamber of our bliss
Might seem a fortress by a haunted main,
Which shouting hosts embattled charge in vain,
Powerless to mar our kiss.

O life, O storm of years,
Our walls are built against your shattering siege;
Our dwelling is with Love, our sovereign liege,
And fenced from change and tears.

SEVERANCE

THE tide falls, and the night falls,
    And the wind blows in from the sea,
And the bell on the bar it calls and calls,
    And the wild hawk cries from his tree.

The late crane calls to his fellows gone
    In long flight over the sea,
And my heart with the crane flies on and on,
    Seeking its rest and thee.

O Love, the tide returns to the strand,
    And the crane flies back oversea,
But he brings not my heart from his far-off land,
    For he brings not thee to me.

EPITAPH FOR A SAILOR BURIED ASHORE

He who but yesterday would roam
    Careless as clouds and currents range,
In homeless wandering most at home,
    Inhabiter of change;

Who wooed the west to win the east,
    And named the stars of North and South,
And felt the zest of Freedom's feast
    Familiar in his mouth;

Who found a faith in stranger-speech,
    And fellowship in foreign hands,
And had within his eager reach
    The relish of all lands—

How circumscribed a plot of earth
    Keeps now his restless footsteps still,
Whose wish was wide as ocean's girth,
    Whose will the water's will!

THE SILVER THAW

THERE came a day of showers
  Upon the shrinking snow ;
The south wind sighed of flowers,
  The softening skies hung low.
Midwinter for a space
Foreshadowing April's face,
The white world caught the fancy,
  And would not let it go.

In reawakened courses
  The brooks rejoiced the land ;
We dreamed the Spring's shy forces
  Were gathering close at hand.
The dripping buds were stirred,
As if the sap had heard
The long-desired persuasion
  Of April's soft command.

But antic Time had cheated
    With hope's elusive gleam ;
The phantom Spring, defeated,
    Fled down the ways of dream.
And in the night the reign
Of winter came again,
With frost upon the forest
    And stillness on the stream.

When morn in rose and crocus
    Came up the bitter sky,
Celestial beams awoke us
    To wondering ecstasy.
The wizard Winter's spell
Had wrought so passing well,
That earth was bathed in glory,
    As if God's smile were nigh.

The silvered saplings, bending,
    Flashed in a rain of gems ;
The statelier trees, attending,
    Blazed in their diadems.

White fire and amethyst
All common things had kissed,
And chrysolites and sapphires
Adorned the bramble-stems.

In crystalline confusion
All beauty came to birth;
It was a kind illusion
To comfort waiting earth—
To bid the buds forget
The Spring so distant yet,
And hearts no more remember
The iron season's dearth.

THE LILY OF THE VALLEY

Did Winter, letting fall in vain regret
   A tear among the tender leaves of May,
Embalm the tribute, lest she might forget,
   In this elect, imperishable way?

Or did the virgin Spring sweet vigil keep
   In the white radiance of the midnight hour,
And whisper to the unwondering ear of Sleep
   Some shy desire that turned into a flower?

THE NIGHT-HAWK

WHEN frogs make merry the pools of May,
    And sweet, oh sweet,
    Through the twilight dim
    Is the vesper hymn
Their myriad mellow pipes repeat
  As the rose-dusk dies away.
  Then hark, the night-hawk!
    (For now is the elfin hour.)
  With melting skies o'er him,
All summer before him,
His wild brown mate to adore him,
    By the spell of his power
    He summons the apples in flower.

In the high pale heaven he flits and calls ;
    Then swift, oh swift,
    On sounding wing
    That hums like a string,

To the quiet glades where the gnat-clouds drift
And the night-moths flicker, he falls.
Then hark, the night-hawk!
 (For now is the elfin hour.)
With melting skies o'er him,
All summer before him,
His wild brown mate to adore him,
 By the spell of his power
 He summons the apples in flower.

THE HERMIT-THRUSH

OVER the tops of the trees,
   And over the shallow stream,
The shepherd of sunset frees
   The amber phantoms of dream.
The time is the time of vision ;
   The hour is the hour of calm ;
Hark ! On the stillness Elysian
   Breaks how divine a psalm !
      Oh, clear in the sphere of the air,
      Clear, clear, tender and far,
      Our aspiration of prayer
      Unto eve's clear star !

O singer serene, secure !
   From thy throat of silver and dew
What transport lonely and pure,
   Unchanging, endlessly new,—

An unremembrance of mirth,
   And a contemplation of tears,
As if the musing of earth
   Communed with the dreams of the years !
     Oh, clear in the sphere of the air,
       Clear, clear, tender and far,
     Our aspiration of prayer
       Unto eve's clear star !

O cloistral ecstatic ! thy cell
   In the cool green aisles of the leaves
Is the shrine of a power by whose spell
   Whoso hears aspires and believes !
O hermit of evening ! thine hour
   Is the sacrament of desire,
When love hath a heavenlier flower,
   And passion a holier fire !
     Oh, clear in the sphere of the air,
       Clear, clear, tender and far,
     Our aspiration of prayer
       Unto eve's clear star !

THE WILD-ROSE THICKET

WHERE humming flies frequent, and where
Pink petals open to the air,

The wild-rose thicket seems to be
The summer in epitome.

Amid its gold-green coverts meet
The late dew and the noonday heat;

Around it, to the sea-rim harsh,
The patient levels of the marsh;

And o'er it the pale heavens bent,
Half sufferance and half content.

MY TREES

At evening, when the winds are still,
    And wide the yellowing landscape glows,
My firwoods on the lonely hill
    Are crowned with sun and loud with crows.
Their flocks throng down the open sky
    From far salt flats and sedgy seas ;
Then dusk and dewfall quench the cry,—
    So calm a home is in my trees.

At morning, when the young wind swings
    The green slim tops and branches high,
Out puffs a noisy whirl of wings,
    Dispersing up the empty sky.
In this dear refuge no roof stops
    The skyward pinion winnowing through.
My trees shut out the world ;—their tops
    Are open to the infinite blue.

THE HAWKBIT

How sweetly on the Autumn scene,
When haws are red amid the green,
The hawkbit shines with face of cheer,
The favourite of the faltering year !

When days grow short and nights grow cold
How fairly gleams its eye of gold,
On pastured field and grassy hill,
Along the roadside and the rill !

It seems the spirit of a flower,
This offspring of the Autumn hour,
Wandering back to earth to bring
Some kindly afterthought of Spring.

A dandelion's ghost might so
Amid Elysian meadows blow,
Become more fragile and more fine
Breathing the atmosphere divine.

GREY ROCKS AND GREYER SEA

Grey rocks, and greyer sea,
   And surf along the shore—
And in my heart a name
   My lips shall speak no more.

The high and lonely hills
   Endure the darkening year—
And in my heart endure
   A memory and a tear.

Across the tide a sail
   That tosses, and is gone—
And in my heart the kiss
   That longing dreams upon.

Grey rocks, and greyer sea,
   And surf along the shore—
And in my heart the face
   That I shall see no more.

A SONG OF CHEER

The winds are up with wakening day
   And tumult in the tree;
Across the cool and open sky
   White clouds are streaming free;
The new light breaks o'er flood and field
   Clear like an echoing horn,
While in loud flight the crows are blown
   Athwart the sapphire morn.

What tho' the maple's scarlet flame
   Declares the summer done,
Tho' finch and starling voyage south
   To win a softer sun,
What tho' the withered leaf whirls by
   To strew the purpling stream,—
Stretched are the world's glad veins with strength.
   Despair is grown a dream!

A SONG OF CHEER

The acres of the golden rod
　Are glorious on the hills.
Tho storm and loss approach, the year's
　High heart upleaps and thrills.
Dearest, the cheer, the brave delight,
　Are given to shame regret.
That when the long frost falls, our hearts
　Be glad, and not forget !

A SONG OF GROWTH

In the heart of a man
   Is a thought upfurled,
Reached its full span
   It shakes the world,
And to one high thought
Is a whole race wrought.

Not with vain noise
   The great work grows,
Nor with foolish voice,
   But in repose,—
Not in the rush
But in the hush.

From the cogent lash
   Of the cloud-herd wind
The low clouds dash,
   Blown headlong, blind :
But beyond, the great blue
Looks moveless through.

A SONG OF GROWTH

O'er the loud world sweep
   The scourge and the rod;
But in deep beyond deep
   Is the stillness of God;
At the Fountains of Life
No cry, no strife.

TO G. B. R.

How merry sings the aftermath,
    With crickets fifing in the dew !
The home-sweet sounds, the scene, the hour,
    I consecrate to you.

All this you knew and loved with me ;
    All this in our delight had part ;
And now—though us earth sees no more
    As comrades, heart to heart—

This kindly strength of open fields,
    This faith of eve, this calm of air,
They lift my spirit close to you
    In memory and prayer.

THE BIRD'S SONG, THE SUN, AND THE WIND

The bird's song, the sun, and the wind
    The wind that rushes, the sun that is still,
The song of the bird that sings alone,
    And wide light washing the lonely hill !

The Spring's coming, the buds and the brooks—
    The brooks that clamour, the buds in the rain,
The coming of Spring that comes unprayed for,
    And eyes that welcome it not for pain !

OH, PURPLE HANG THE PODS

Oh, purple hang the pods
   On the green locust-tree,
And yellow turn the sods
   On a grave that's dear to me!

And blue, softly blue,
   The hollow Autumn sky,
With its birds flying through
   To where the sun-lands lie!

In the sun-lands they'll bide
   While Winter's on the tree;—
And oh that I might hide
   The grave that's dear to me!

BRINGING HOME THE COWS

When potatoes were in blossom,
   When the new hay filled the mows,
Sweet the paths we trod together,
   Bringing home the cows.

What a purple kissed the pasture,
   Kissed and blessed the alder-boughs,
As we wandered slow at sundown,
   Bringing home the cows!

How the far-off hills were gilded
   With the light that dream allows,
As we built our hopes beyond them,
   Bringing home the cows!

How our eyes were bright with visions,
   What a meaning wreathed our brows,
As we watched the cranes, and lingered,
   Bringing home the cows!

Past the years, and through the distance,
  Throbs the memory of our vows.
Oh that we again were children
  Bringing home the cows !

THE KEEPERS OF THE PASS

[When the Iroquois were moving in overwhelming force to obliterate the infant town of Montreal, Adam Daulac and a small band of comrades, binding themselves by oath not to return alive, went forth to meet the enemy in a distant pass between the Ottawa river and the hills. There they died to a man, but not till they had slain so many of the savages that the invading force was shattered and compelled to withdraw.]

Now heap the branchy barriers up.
    No more for us shall burn
The pine-logs on the happy hearth,
    For we shall not return.

We've come to our last camping-ground.
    Set axe to fir and tamarack.
The foe is here, the end is near,
    And we shall not turn back.

In vain for us the town shall wait,
    The home-dear faces yearn,
The watchers on the steeple watch,—
    For we shall not return.

For them we're come to these hard straits,
  To save from flame and wrack
The little city built far off;
  And we shall not turn back.

Now beat the yelling butchers down.
  Let musket blaze, and axe-edge burn.
Set hand to hand, lay brand to brand,
  But we shall not return.

For every man of us that falls
  Their hordes a score shall lack.
Close in about the Lily Flag!
  No man of us goes back.

For us no morrow's dawn shall break.
  Our sons and wives shall learn
Some day from lips of flying scout
  Why we might not return.

A dream of children's laughter comes
  Across the battle's slack,
A vision of familiar streets,—
  But we shall not go back.

Up roars the painted storm once more.
  Long rest we soon shall earn.
Henceforth the city safe may sleep,
  But we shall not return.

And when our last has fallen in blood
  Between these waters black,
Their tribe shall no more lust for war,—
  For we shall not turn back.

In vain for us the town shall wait,
  The home-dear faces yearn,
The watchers in the steeple watch,
  For we shall not return.

NEW YEAR'S EVE

(AFTER THE FRENCH OF FRÉCHETTE)

YE night winds shaking the weighted boughs
    Of snow-blanched hemlock and frosted fir,
While crackles sharply the thin crust under
    The passing feet of the wayfarer;

Ye night cries pulsing in long-drawn waves
    Where beats the bitter tide to its flood;
A tumult of pain, a rumour of sorrow,
    Troubling the starred night's tranquil mood;

Ye shudderings where, like a great beast bound,
    The forest strains to its depths remote;
Be still and hark! From the high gray tower
    The great bell sobs in its brazen throat.

NEW YEAR'S EVE

A strange voice out of the pallid heaven,
   Twelve sobs it utters, and stops. Midnight!
'Tis the ominous *Hail!* and the stern *Farewell!*
   Of Past and Present in passing flight.

This moment, herald of hope and doom,
   That cries in our ears and then is gone,
Has marked for us in the awful volume
   One step toward the infinite dark—or dawn!

A year is gone, and a year begins.
   Ye wise ones, knowing in Nature's scheme,
Oh tell us whither they go, the years
   That drop in the gulfs of time and dream!

They go to the goal of all things mortal,
   Where fade our destinies, scarce perceived,
To the dim abyss wherein time confounds them—
   The hours we laughed and the days we grieved.

They go where the bubbles of rainbow break
   We breathed in our youth of love and fame,
Where great and small are as one together,
   And oak and windflower counted the same.

They go where follow our smiles and tears,
  The gold of youth and the gray of age,
Where falls the storm and falls the stillness,
  The laughter of spring and winter's rage.

What hand shall gauge the depth of time
  Or a little measure eternity?
God only, as they unroll before Him,
  Conceives and orders the mystery.

A CHRISTMAS-EVE COURTIN'

THE snow'd laid deep that winter from the middle of November;
The goin', as I remember, was the purtiest kind of goin';
An' as the time drawed nigh fur turkeys an' mince pie
The woods, all white an' frosted, was a sight worth showin'.

The snow hung down the woodpiles all scalloped-l'ke an' curled.
You'd swear in all the world ther' warn't no fences any more.
The cows kep' under cover, an' the chickens scratched twice over
The yaller ruck of straw a-layin' round the stable door.

"Twas Christmas Eve, in the afternoon, an' the store was jest a-hummin'
When we seen the parson comin' in his pung along the road;

An' as he passed the store he called in through the door.
'Church to-night at the Crossroads ! Come, boys, and bring a load !'

'Twas a new idee in them parts, an' Bill Simmons made 'n oration
About 'High Church innovation,' an' 'a-driftin' back to Rome,'
But I backed the parson's rights to have Church o' moonlight nights ;
An' I thought of Nance's cute red lips, an' pinted straight fur home.

I wasn't long a-gittin' the chores done up, you bet,
An' the supper that I eat wouldn't more'n a' fed a fly !
Then I hitched the mare in the pung an' soon was bowlin' along
Down by the crick to Nance's while the moon was white an' high.

She didn't keep me waitin', fur church was at half-pas' seven ;
An' my idee of Heaven, as I tucked her into the furs,

Was a-ridin' with Nance at night when the moon was high
    an' white,
An' the deep sky all a-sparkle like them laughin' eyes of
    hers.

I had a heap to say, but I couldn't jest find my tongue ;
But my heart it sung an' sung, like canaries was into it.
So I chirruped to the mare with a kind of easy air,
An' Nance had to do the talkin',—as was jest the one
    could do it !

An' I could feel her shoulder, kind of comfortin' an'
    warm,
Nestlin' agin my arm,—sech a sweet an' cunnin' shoulder.
My heart was all afire, but I kep' gittin' shyer an' shyer,
An' wished that I'd been born a leetle sassier an' bolder.

We come to them there Crossroads 'fore I'd time to say
    a word ;
An' I reckon as how I heard mighty little of the sarvice.
But 'twas grand to hear Nance sing ' Glory to the new-
    born King,'
Tho' the way the choir folks stared at us, it made me kind
    of narvous.

I wished the parson'd stop an' give me another chance
Out there in the night with Nance, under the stars an' moon;
An' I vowed I'd have my say in the tidiest kind of way,
An' she shouldn't have no more call to think me a blame gossoon.

At last the preachin' come to an end, an' the folks all crowded out.
'Fore I knowed what I was about we was on the road fur home.
But the sky was overcast an' a thick snow droppin' fast,
An' a big wind down from the mountins got a-rantin' an moanin' some.

We hadn't rode two mile when it blowed like all possessed,
An' at that I kind of guessed we was in fur a ticklish night.
We couldn't go more'n a walk, an' Nance she forgot to talk;
Then I jest slipped my arm around her, an' she never kicked a mite.

Well, now, if the hull blame roof'd blowed off I wouldn't
    'a keered,
But I seen as how Nance was skeered, so I sez, 'By
    gracious, Nance,
I guess if we don't turn, an' cut back for the Crossroads,
    durn
The shelter we'll git to-night by any kind of a chance !'

Then the mare stopped short an' whinnied, an' Nance
    jest said, 'Oh, Si !'
An' then commenced to cry, till I felt like cryin' too ;
I forgot about the storm, an' jest hugged her close an'
    warm,
An' kissed her, an' kissed her, an' swore as how I'd be true.

Then Nance she quit her cryin' an' said she wastn't
    skeered
So long's she knowed I keered jest a leetle mite fur her ;
But she guessed we'd better try an' git home, an' ' by-
    an'-by
The storm 'll stop, an' anyways, it ain't so very fur !'

My heart was that chock full I couldn't find a word to
    say,
But she understood the way that I looked into her eyes !

In buffaler robe an' rug I wrapped her warm an' snug,
An' got out an' broke the mare a road all the way to
    Barnes's Rise.

'Twas a tallish tramp, I tell you, a-leadin' that flounderin'
    mare
Thro' snow drifts anywheres from four to six foot deep.
An' a 'painter' now an' then howled out from his moun-
    tin den ;
But Nance, she never heered it, fur she must 'a fell to
    sleep.

It wasn't fur from mornin' when we come to Barnes's
    Rise,—
An' I found to my surprise I'd tramped nine mile an'
    wasn't tired.
I was in sech a happy dream it didn't hardly seem
As the ride had been any tougher'n jest what I'd desired.

It was easier goin' now, an' Nance woke up all rosy.
She was sweeter'n any posy as I kissed her at the gate.
The dawn was jest a-growin' so I wished her a Merry
    Christmas,
An' remarked I must be goin' as it might be gittin' late !

We was married at the Crossroads jest six weeks from
    Christmas Eve ;
An' Nance an' me believe in our parson's innovations ;
We ain't much skeered o' Rome, an' we reckon he can
    preach some,
An' we call that evenin' sarvice a Providential Dispen-
    sation.

THE SUCCOUR OF GLUSKÂP

(A MICMAC LEGEND)

THE happy valley laughed with sun,
　The corn grew firm in stalk,
The lodges clustered safe where run
　The streams of Peniawk.

The washing-pools and shallows rang
　With shout of lads at play ;
At corn-hoeing the women sang ;
　The warriors were away.

The splashed white pebbles on the beach,
　The idling paddles, gleamed ;
Before the lodge doors, spare of speech,
　The old men basked and dreamed.

And when the windless noon grew hot,
　And the white sun beat like steel,
In shade about the shimmering pot
　They gathered to their meal.

Then from the hills, on flying feet,
    A desperate runner came,
With cry that smote the peaceful street,
    And slew the peace with shame.

"Trapped in the night, and snared in sleep,
    Our warriors wake no more!
Up from Wahloos the Mohawks creep—
    Their feet are at the door!"

The grey old sachems rose and mocked
    The ruin that drew near;
And down the beach the children flocked,
    And women wild with fear.

Launched were the red canoes; when, lo!
    Beside them Gluskâp stood,
Appearing with his giant bow
    From out his mystic wood.

With quiet voice he called them back,
    And comforted their fears;
He swore the lodges should not lack,
    He dried the children's tears;

Till sorrowing mothers almost deemed
    The desperate runner lied,
And the tired children slept, and dreamed
    Their fathers had not died.

That night behind the mystic wood
    The Mohawk warriors crept;
A spell went through the solitude
    And stilled them, and they slept.

And when the round moon, rising late,
    The Hills of Kawlm had crossed,
She saw the camp of Mohawk hate
    Swathed in a great white frost.

At morn, behind the mystic wood
    Came Gluskâp, bow in hand,
And marked the ice-bound solitude,
    And that unwaking band.

But as he gazed his lips grew mild,
    For, safe among the dead,
There played a ruddy, laughing child
    By a captive mother's head;

And child and mother, nestling warm,
    Scarce knew their foes had died,
As past their sleep the noiseless storm
    Of strange death turned aside.

HOW THE MOHAWKS SET OUT FOR MEDOCTEC

[When the invading Mohawks captured the outlying Melicite village of Madawaska, they spared two squaws to guide them down stream to the main Melicite town of Medoctec, below Grand Falls. The squaws steered themselves and their captors over the Falls.]

I

Grows the great deed, though none
Shout to behold it done !
To the brave deed done by night
Heaven testifies in the light

Stealthy and swift as a dream,
Crowding the breast of the stream,
In their paint and plumes of war
And their war-canoes four score,

They are threading the Oolastook,
Where his cradling hills o'erlook.
The branchy thickets hide them ;
The unstartled waters guide them.

II

Comes night to the quiet hills
Where the Madawaska spills,—
To his slumbering huts no warning,
Nor mirth of another morning !

No more shall the children wake
As the dawns through the hut-door break;
But the dogs, a trembling pack,
With wistful eyes steal back.

And, to pilot the noiseless foe
Through the perilous passes, go
Two women who could not die—
Whom the knife in the dark passed by.

III

Where the shoaling waters froth,
Churned thick like devils' broth,—
Where the rocky shark-jaw waits,
Never a bark that grates.

And the tearless captives' skill
Contents them. Onward still !
And the low-voiced captives tell
The tidings that cheer them well :

How a clear stream leads them down
Well-nigh to Medoctec town,
Ere to the great Falls' thunder
The long wall yawns asunder.

IV

The clear stream glimmers before them ;
The faint night falters o'er them ;
Lashed lightly bark to bark,
They glide the windless dark.

Late grows the night. No fear
While the skilful captives steer !
Sleeps the tired warrior, sleeps
The chief; and the river creeps.

V

In the town of the Melicite
The unjarred peace is sweet,
Green grows the corn and great,
And the hunt is fortunate.

This many a heedless year
The Mohawks come not near.
The lodge-gate stands unbarred ;
Scarce even a dog keeps guard.

No mother shrieks from a dream
Of blood on the threshold stream,—
But the thought of those mute guides
Is where the sleeper bides !

VI

Gets forth those caverned walls
No roar from the giant Falls,
Whose mountainous foam treads under
The abyss of awful thunder.

But—the river's sudden speed !
How the ghost-grey shores recede !
And the tearless pilots hear
A muttering voice creep near.

A tremor ! The blanched waves leap.
The warriors start from sleep.
Faints in the sudden blare
The cry of their swift despair,

And the captives' death-chant shrills . . .
But afar, remote from ills,
Quiet under the quiet skies
The Melicite village lies.

THE WOOD FROLIC

THE Morning Star was bitter bright, the morning sky was grey ;
And we hitched our teams and started for the woods at break of day.
    Oh, the frost is on the forest, and the snow piles high !

Along the white and winding road the sled-bells jangled keen
Between the buried fences, the billowy drifts between.
    Oh, merry swing the axes, and the bright chips fly !

So crisp sang the runners, and so swift the horses sped,
That the woods were all about us ere the sky grew red.
    Oh, the frost is on the forest, and the snow piles high !

The bark hung ragged on the birch, the lichen on the fir,
The lungwort fringed the maple, and grey moss the juniper.
    Oh, merry swing the axes, and the bright chips fly !

So still the air and chill the air the branches seemed
  asleep,
But we broke their ancient visions as the axe bit deep.
  Oh, the frost is on the forest, and the snow piles high !

With the shouts of the choppers and the barking of their
  blades,
How rang the startled valleys and the rabbit-haunted
  glades !
  Oh, merry swing the axes, and the bright chips fly !

The hard wood and the soft wood, we felled them for
  our use ;
And chiefly, for its scented gum, we loved the scaly
  spruce ;
  Oh, the frost is on the forest, and the snow piles high !

And here and there, with solemn roar, some hoary tree
  came down,
And we heard the rolling of the years in the thunder of
  its crown.
  Oh, merry swing the axes, and the bright chips fly !

So, many a sled was loaded up above the stake-tops soon ;
And many a load was at the farm before the horn of noon ;
Oh, the frost is on the forest, and the snow piles high !

And ere we saw the sundown all yellow through the trees,
The farmyard stood as thick with wood as a buckwheat patch with bees ;
Oh, merry swing the axes, and the bright chips fly !

And with the last-returning teams, and axes burnished bright,
We left the woods to slumber in the frosty shadowed night.
Oh, the frost is on the forest, and the snow piles high !

And then the wide, warm kitchen, with beams across the ceiling,
Thick hung with red-skinned onions, and homely herbs of healing !
Oh, merry swing the axes, and the bright chips fly !

The dishes on the dresser-shelves were shining blue and
  white,
And o'er the loaded table the lamps beamed bright.
  Oh, the frost is on the forest, and the snow piles high!

Then, how the ham and turkey and the apple-sauce did
  fly,
The heights of boiled potatoes and the flats of pumpkin-
  pie!
  Oh, merry swing the axes, and the bright chips fly!

With bread-and-cheese and doughnuts fit to feed a farm
  a year!
And we washed them down with tides of tea and oceans
  of spruce beer.
  Oh, the frost is on the forest, and the snow piles high!

At last the pipes were lighted and the chairs pushed
  back,
And Bill struck up a sea-song on a rather risky tack;
  Oh, merry swing the axes, and the bright chips fly!

And the girls all thought it funny—but they never knew
  'twas worse,
For we gagged him with a doughnut at the famous second
  verse.
  Oh, the frost is on the forest, and the snow piles high !

Then someone fetched a fiddle, and we shoved away the
  table,
And 'twas jig and reel and polka just as long as we were
  able,
  Oh, merry swing the axes, and the bright chips fly !

Till at last the girls grew sleepy, and we got our coats to
  go.
We started off with racing-teams and moonlight on the
  snow;
  Oh, the frost is on the forest, and the snow piles high !

And soon again the winter world was voiceless as of old,
Alone with all the wheeling stars, and the great white
  cold.
  Oh, the frost is on the forest, and the snow piles high !

CANADIAN STREAMS

O RIVERS rolling to the sea
From lands that bear the maple-tree,
   How swell your voices with the strain
Of loyalty and liberty !

A holy music, heard in vain
By coward heart and sordid brain,
   To whom this strenuous being seems
Naught but a greedy race for gain.

O unsung streams — not splendid themes
Ye lack to fire your patriot dreams !
   Annals of glory gild your waves,
Hope freights your tides, Canadian streams !

St. Lawrence, whose wide water laves
The shores that ne'er have nourished slaves !
   Swift Richelieu of lilied fame !
Niagara of glorious graves !

Thy rapids, Ottawa, proclaim
Where Daulac and his heroes came !
   Thy tides, St. John, declare La Tour,
And, later, many a loyal name !

Thou inland stream, whose vales, secure
From storm, Tecumseh's death made poor !
   And thou small water, red with war,
'Twixt Beaubassin and Beauséjour !

Dread Saguenay, where eagles soar,
What voice shall from the bastioned shore
   The tale of Roberval reveal,
Or his mysterious fate deplore ?

Annapolis, do thy floods yet feel
Faint memories of Champlain's keel,
   Thy pulses yet the deed repeat
Of Poutrincourt and d'Iberville ?

And thou far tide, whose plains now beat
With march of myriad westering feet,
   Saskatchewan, whose virgin sod
So late Canadian blood made sweet ?

Your bulwark hills, your valleys broad,
Streams where de Salaberry trod,
   Where Wolfe achieved, where Brock was slain,
Their voices are the voice of God !

O sacred waters ! not in vain,
Across Canadian height and plain,
   Ye sound us in triumphant tone
The summons of your high refrain.

AVE!

AVE!

AN ODE FOR THE CENTENARY OF SHELLEY'S BIRTH

I

O TRANQUIL meadows, grassy Tantramar,
  Wide marshes ever washed in clearest air,
Whether beneath the sole and spectral star
  The dear severity of dawn you wear,
Or whether in the joy of ample day
  And speechless ecstasy of growing June
You lie and dream the long blue hours away
    Till nightfall comes too soon,
Or whether, naked to the unstarred night,
You strike with wondering awe my inward sight,—

II

You know how I have loved you, how my dreams
  Go forth to you with longing, though the years
That turn not back like your returning streams
  And fain would mist the memory with tears,

Though the inexorable years deny
   My feet the fellowship of your deep grass,
O'er which, as o'er another, tenderer sky,
   Cloud phantoms drift and pass,—
You know my confident love, since first, a child,
Amid your wastes of green I wandered wild.

III

Inconstant, eager, curious, I roamed ;
   And ever your long reaches lured me on ;
And ever o'er my feet your grasses foamed,
   And in my eyes your far horizons shone.
But sometimes would you (as a stillness fell
   And on my pulse you laid a soothing palm),
Instruct my ears in your most secret spell ;
   And sometimes in the calm
Initiate my young and wondering eyes
Until my spirit grew more still and wise.

IV

Purged with high thoughts and infinite desire
   I entered fearless the most holy place,
Received between my lips the secret fire,
   The breath of inspiration on my face.

But not for long these rare illumined hours,
  The deep surprise and rapture not for long.
Again I saw the common, kindly flowers,
    Again I heard the song
Of the glad bobolink, whose lyric throat
Pealed like a tangle of small bells afloat.

V

The pounce of mottled marsh-hawk on his prey :
  The flicker of sand-pipers in from sea
In gusty flocks that puffed and fled ; the play
  Of field-mice in the vetches ;—these to me
Were memorable events. But most availed
  Your strange unquiet waters to engage
My kindred heart's companionship ; nor failed
    To grant this heritage,—
That in my veins for ever must abide
The urge and fluctuation of the tide.

VI

The mystic river whence you take your name,
  River of hubbub, raucous Tantramar,
Untamable and changeable as flame,
  It called me and compelled me from afar,

Shaping my soul with its impetuous stress.
   When in its gaping channel deep withdrawn
Its waves ran crying of the wilderness
     And winds and stars and dawn,
How I companioned them in speed sublime,
Led out a vagrant on the hills of Time !

VII

And when the orange flood came roaring in
   From Fundy's tumbling troughs and tide-worn caves,
While red Minudie's flats were drowned with din
   And rough Chignecto's front oppugned the waves,
How blithely with the refluent foam I raced
   Inland along the radiant chasm, exploring
The green solemnity with boisterous haste ;
     My pulse of joy outpouring
To visit all the creeks that twist and shine
From Beauséjour to utmost Tormentine.

VIII

And after, when the tide was full, and stilled
   A little while the seething and the hiss,
And every tributary channel filled
   To the brim with rosy streams that swelled to kiss

The grass-roots all a-wash and goose-tongue wild
And salt-sap rosemary,—then how well content
I was to rest me like a breathless child
    With play-time rapture spent,—
To lapse and loiter till the change should come
And the great floods turn seaward, roaring home.

IX

And now, O tranquil marshes, in your vast
    Serenity of vision and of dream,
Wherethrough by every intricate vein have passed
    With joy impetuous and pain supreme
The sharp fierce tides that chafe the shores of earth
    In endless and controlless ebb and flow,
Strangely akin you seem to him whose birth
    One hundred years ago
With fiery succour to the ranks of song
Defied the ancient gates of wrath and wrong.

X

Like yours, O marshes, his compassionate breast,
    Wherein abode all dreams of love and peace,
Was tortured with perpetual unrest.
    Now loud with flood, now languid with release,

Now poignant with the lonely ebb, the strife
    Of tides from the salt sea of human pain
That hiss along the perilous coasts of life
    Beat in his eager brain;
But all about the tumult of his heart
Stretched the great calm of his celestial art.

XI

Therefore with no far flight, from Tantramar
    And my still world of ecstasy, to thee,
Shelley, to thee I turn, the avatar
    Of Song, Love, Dream, Desire and Liberty;
To thee I turn with reverent hands of prayer
    And lips that fain would ease my heart of praise,
Whom chief of all whose brows prophetic wear
        The pure and sacred bays
I worship, and have worshipped since the hour
When first I felt thy bright and chainless power.

XII

About thy sheltered cradle, in the green
    Untroubled groves of Sussex, brooded forms
That to the mother's eye remained unseen,—
    Terrors and ardours, passionate hopes, and storms

Of fierce retributive fury, such as jarred
    Ancient and sceptred creeds, and cast down kings,
And oft the holy cause of Freedom marred
    With lust of meaner things,
With guiltless blood, and many a frenzied crime
Dared in the face of unforgetful Time.

XIII

The star that burns on revolution smote
    Wild heats and change on thine ascendant sphere,
Whose influence thereafter seemed to float
    Through many a strange eclipse of wrath and fear,
Dimming awhile the radiance of thy love.
    But still supreme in thy nativity,
All dark, invidious aspects far above,
    Beamed one clear orb for thee,—
The star whose ministrations just and strong
Controlled the tireless flight of Dante's song.

XIV

With how august contrition, and what tears
    Of penitential unavailing shame,
Thy venerable foster-mother hears
    The sons of song impeach her ancient name,

Because in one rash hour of anger blind
    She thrust thee forth in exile, and thy feet
Too soon to earth's wild outer ways consigned,—
    Far from her well-loved seat,
Far from her studious halls and storied towers
And weedy Isis winding through his flowers.

XV

And thou, thenceforth the breathless child of change,
    Thine own Alastor, on an endless quest
Of unimagined loveliness, didst range,
    Urged ever by the soul's divine unrest.
Of that high quest and that unrest divine
    Thy first immortal music thou didst make,
Inwrought with fairy Alp, and Reuss, and Rhine,
    And phantom seas that break
In soundless foam along the shores of Time,
Prisoned in thine imperishable rhyme.

XVI

Thyself the lark melodious in mid-heaven;
    Thyself the Protean shape of chainless cloud,
Pregnant with elemental fire, and driven
    Through deeps of quivering light, and darkness loud

With tempest, yet beneficent as prayer ;
   Thyself the wild west wind, relentless strewing
The withered leaves of custom on the air,
   And through the wreck pursuing
O'er lovelier Arnos, more imperial Romes,
Thy radiant visions to their viewless homes.

XVII

And when thy mightiest creation thou
   Wert fain to body forth,—the dauntless form,
The all-enduring, all-forgiving brow
   Of the great Titan, flinchless in the storm
Of pangs unspeakable and nameless hates,
   Yet rent by all the wrongs and woes of men,
And triumphing in his pain, that so their fates
   Might be assuaged,—oh then
Out of that vast compassionate heart of thine
Thou wert constrained to shape the dream benign.

XVIII

—O Baths of Caracalla, arches clad
   In such transcendent rhapsodies of green
That one might guess the sprites of spring were glad
   For your majestic ruin, yours the scene,

The illuminating air of sense and thought ;
   And yours the enchanted light, O skies of Rome,
Where the giant vision into form was wrought ;
   Beneath your blazing dome
The intensest song our language ever knew
Beat up exhaustless to the blinding blue !—

XIX

The domes of Pisa and her towers superb,
   The myrtles and the ilexes that sigh
O'er San Giuliano, where no jars disturb
   The lonely aziola's evening cry,
The Serchio's sun-kissed waters,—these conspired
   With Plato's theme occult, with Dante's calm
Rapture of mystic love, and so inspired
   Thy soul's espousal psalm,
A strain of such elect and pure intent
It breathes of a diviner element.

XX

Thou on whose lips the word of Love became
   A rapt evangel to assuage all wrong,
Not Love alone, but the austerer name
   Of Death engaged the splendours of thy song.

The luminous grief, the spacious consolation
  Of thy supreme lament, that mourned for him
Too early haled to that still habitation
    Beneath the grass-roots dim,—
Where his faint limbs and pain-o'erwearied heart
Of all earth's loveliness became a part,

XXI

But where, thou sayest, himself would not abide,—
  Thy solemn incommunicable joy
Announcing Adonais has not died,
    Attesting death to free but not destroy,
All this was as thy swan-song mystical.
  Even while the note serene was on thy tongue
Thin grew the veil of the Invisible,
    The white sword nearer swung,—
And in the sudden wisdom of thy rest
Thou knewest all thou hadst but dimly guessed.

XXII

—Lament, Lerici, mourn for the world's loss !
  Mourn that pure light of song extinct at noon !
Ye waves of Spezzia that shine and toss
    Repent that sacred flame you quenched too soon !

Mourn, Mediterranean waters, mourn
   In affluent purple down your golden shore !
Such strains as his, whose voice you stilled in scorn,
   Our ears may greet no more,
Unless at last to that far sphere we climb
Where he completes the wonder of his rhyme !

XXIII

How like a cloud she fled, thy fateful bark,
   From eyes that watched to hearts that waited, till
Up from the ocean roared the tempest dark—
   And the wild heart love waited for was still !
Hither and thither in the slow, soft tide,
   Rolled seaward, shoreward, sands and wandering shells
And shifting weeds thy fellows, thou didst hide
   Remote from all farewells,
Nor felt the sun, nor heard the fleeting rain,
Nor heeded Casa Magni's quenchless pain.

XXIV

Thou heededst not ?   Nay, for it was not thou,
   That blind, mute clay relinquished by the waves
Reluctantly at last, and slumbering now
   In one of kind earth's most compassionate graves !

Not thou, not thou,—for thou wert in the light
   Of the Unspeakable, where time is not.
Thou sawest those tears ; but in thy perfect sight
      And thy eternal thought
Were they not even now all wiped away
In the reunion of the infinite day !

XXV

There face to face thou sawest the living God
   And worshipedst, beholding Him the same
Adored on earth as Love, the same whose rod
   Thou hadst endured as Life, whose secret name
Thou now didst learn, the healing name of Death.
   In that unroutable profound of peace,
Beyond experience of pulse and breath,
      Beyond the last release
Of longing, rose to greet thee all the lords
Of Thought, with consummation in their words.

XXVI

He of the seven cities claimed, whose eyes,
   Though blind, saw gods and heroes, and the fall
Of Ilium, and many alien skies,
   And Circe's Isle ; and he whom mortals call

The Thunderous, who sang the Titan bound
    As thou the Titan victor ; the benign
Spirit of Plato ; Job ; and Judah's crowned
       Singer and seer divine ;
Omar ; the Tuscan ; Milton vast and strong ;
And Shakspeare, captain of the host of Song.

XXVII

Back from the underworld of whelming change
    To the wide-glittering beach thy body came ;
And thou didst contemplate with wonder strange
       And curious regard thy kindred flame,
Fed sweet with frankincense and wine and salt,
    With fierce purgation search thee, soon resolving
Thee to the elements of the airy vault
       And the far spheres revolving,
The common waters, the familiar woods,
And the great hills' inviolate solitudes.

XXVIII

Thy close companions there officiated
    With solemn mourning and with mindful tears ;—
The pained, imperious wanderer unmated
    Who voiced the wrath of those rebellious years ;

Trelawney, lion limbed and high of heart ;
    And he, that gentlest sage and friend most true,
Whom Adonais loved. With these bore part
        One grieving ghost, that flew
Hither and thither through the smoke unstirred
In wailing semblance of a wild white bird.

XXIX

O heart of fire, that fire might not consume,
    For ever glad the world because of thee ;
Because of thee for ever eyes illume
    A more enchanted earth, a lovelier sea !
O poignant voice of the desire of life,
    Piercing our lethargy, because thy call
Aroused our spirits to a nobler strife
        Where base and sordid fall,
For ever past the conflict and the pain
More clearly beams the goal we shall attain !

XXX

And now once more, O marshes, back to you
    From whatsoever wanderings, near or far,
To you I turn with joy for ever new,
    To you, O sovereign vasts of Tantramar !

Your tides are at the full.   Your wizard flood,
   With every tribute stream and brimming creek,
Ponders, possessor of the utmost good,
   With no more left to seek ;—
But the hour wanes and passes ; and once more
Resounds the ebb with destiny in its roar.

XXXI

So might some lord of men, whom force and fate
   And his great heart's unvanquishable power
Have thrust with storm to his supreme estate,
   Ascend by night his solitary tower
High o'er the city's lights and cries uplift.
   Silent he ponders the scrolled heaven to read
And the keen stars' conflicting message sift,
   Till the slow signs recede,
And ominously scarlet dawns afar
The day he leads his legions forth to war.

PRINTED BY
SPOTTISWOODE AND CO., NEW-STREET SQUARE
LONDON

www.ingramcontent.com/pod-product-compliance
Lightning Source LLC
Chambersburg PA
CBHW022131160426
43197CB00009B/1236